"He is in your fire."

Little Sparrow Ministries

Copyright @ 2017 by Little Sparrow Ministries
All Rights Reserved
Printed in the United States of America
International Standard Book Number:
978-1-5323-1912-9

Little Sparrow Ministries
P.O. Box 307
Lindale, Texas 75771
E-mail: lsparrowministries@gmail.com

Web site: http://www.littlesparrowministries.com

Co-Authors: Our Lord and Savior Jesus Christ
Judy H. Farris-Smith, Servant of God

No part of this book may be reproduced or transmitted in any form or by any means, electronic or mechanical, including photocopying, recording, or by any information storage and retrieval system, without permission in writing from Little Sparrow Ministries.

Scripture quotations are taken from the HOLY BIBLE, NEW INTERNATIONAL VERSION®. NIV®. Copyright© 1973, 1978, 1984 by International Bible Society. Used by permission of Zondervan. All rights reserved.

**INGRAM BOOK COMPANY
DISTRIBUTORS**

STORY OF THE COVER

I had been ill for several years, and the doctors could not find the cause of my illness. After seeing countless doctors, I was depressed; I wanted to give up. At times, I would feel that my time on this earth was very short.

I prayed and pleaded with the Lord, but nothing happened. I want you to know that in the past, He has healed me many times. I could not understand why I was not healed.

For several days, I saw a vision of a fire and a cross inside the fire. I asked the Lord if he wanted me to paint it. The answer was, "Yes." As you can see, I painted the vision, and it became the cover of this book. The Lord told me that, "He was in the middle of my fire."

A week or so later, I found out what was causing my illness. I am now recovering. Read: Daniel 3: 19-28. Remember: He is in the middle of your fire also!

Judy H. Farris-Smith

DEALING WITH THE TRAUMA

We, as God's people, are constantly wrestling with forces of darkness. Ephesians 6:12 states: *"For our struggle is not against flesh and blood, but against the rulers, against the authorities, against the powers of this dark world, and against the spiritual forces of evil in the heavenly realm."*

Sometimes getting healed depends on our willingness to use our God-given authority. We must resist the enemy: renounce him; renounce our participation in his wicked plans and schemes; confess our sins; and forgive those who have hurt and offended us.

When we do not have complete control of our minds due to trauma, the enemy can enter into our thought processes. When I had trauma, I remember certain ideas and thoughts would enter into my thought processes; I knew they were not from God. I fought against them continually until the day I was set free.

My Christian counselor told me that she would try to help me on one condition. That one condition was not to take any sort of medication. I was to face my emotional pain and deal with it. If at all possible, I would advise you to do the same thing.

Dealing with this illness will not be easy. Trauma happens. It could be due to serving in the military, accidents, deaths, or abuse. There are many other causes. Whatever the cause, God wants to heal you. Nothing is impossible with Him.

Lean on Him, and talk to Him. He will direct you through this process. He directed me, and He will direct you. I am free, and you will be free also.

Before we begin, take some time and make a list of all the people who have wounded you. Go back to your childhood. Also, please write down all events that may have caused you pain and, therefore, trauma. Ask the Lord to help you.

Judith H. Farris-Smith

PRAYER OF SALVATION

If you have not asked our Lord Jesus Christ into your heart, please do so now. He is waiting to take you out of darkness and into the light.

Lord Jesus, forgive my sins. I confess you to be the Christ, the Son of the living God, and I receive you as my Lord and Savior. Thank you for washing my sins away with your blood and for giving me the gift of your Holy Spirit. Amen

WATER BAPTISM

In Acts 22:16, it states *"And now what are you waiting for? Get up, be baptized and wash your sins away, calling on his name."* It is clear that water baptism after believing in Jesus is a commandment. As soon as you believe in Jesus and repent, you are to be baptized.

The word baptism in the New Testament is bap-tid-zo and bap-tis-mos. These words mean fully wet; technique of the ordinance of Christ; to wash away; to immerse or dip under water. Jesus was baptized fully wet. The disciples were baptized fully wet. In baptism, we are identifying with Christ's death and resurrection.

Matthew 28:19-20 *Therefore, go and make disciples of all nations, baptizing them in the name of the Father and of the Son and of the Holy Spirit...*

Acts 2:38 *Repent and be baptized every one of you in the name of Jesus Christ for the forgiveness of your sins. And you will receive the gift of the Holy Spirit.*

It is the public profession of faith and discipleship. Baptism signifies:

- A confession of faith in Christ;
- A cleansing or washing of the soul from sin;
- A death to sin and a new life in righteousness.

HOLY SPIRIT BAPTISM

John 7:38 *Whoever believes in me, as the scripture has said, streams of living water will flow from within him.*

Acts 2:17-18 *In the last days, God says, I will pour out my Spirit on all people. Your sons and daughters will prophesy, your young men will see visions, your old men will dream dreams. Even on my servants, both men and women, I will pour out my Spirit in those days; and they will prophesy.*

What is the purpose of the Baptism of the Holy Spirit?

1. Giving thanks   1 Corinthians 14:15-17

2. Worshipping   Acts 2:11

3. Empowerment for service   Acts 1:8

The baptism of the Holy Spirit is evidenced by the speaking of tongues. *"For anyone who speaks in a tongue does not speak to men but to God."* (1 Corinthians 14:2) This is a permanent gift given to you by the Holy Spirit.

Acts 1:8 *But you shall receive power when the Holy Spirit comes on you; and you will be my witnesses in*

Jerusalem, and in all Judea and Samaria and to the end of the earth.

The Lord <u>commanded</u> us to receive the baptism of the Holy Spirit. How do I receive the baptism of the Holy Spirit? You receive this baptism by faith simply asking God for it. Prayer to receive the baptism of the Holy Spirit:

Lord Jesus, I thank you for dying on the cross for my sins and for being my Lord and Savior. I ask you to baptize me with your Holy Spirit; I ask you to empower me to be of service and to have the gift of speaking to you in other tongues. Thank you, Lord. Amen.

Matthew 3:11 *I baptize you with water for repentance. But after me will come one who is more powerful than I, whose sandals I am not fit to carry. He will baptize you with the Holy Spirit and with fire.*

(Do not be discouraged if the language does not come immediately. It may come while you are in the shower or riding in your automobile. Just continue to praise our Lord Jesus Christ, and you will begin to see change in your life.

Read the books of Acts and 1 Corinthians. The word and Jesus will become more real in the coming weeks.)

TABLE OF CONTENTS

PART 1 1
Beginning Prayer 2
Deception..3
Spirit of Offense 5
Forgiveness...12
Root of Bitterness.......................................14
Releasing Ungodly Soul-Ties..................20
Prayer to Restore our Fragmented Souls.23
Testimony..25

PART II 31
Generational Curses 32
Prayers for Breaking Gen. Curses...........38
Occult Practices Inventory 41
Occult Practices Prayers...........................43
Additional Deliverance Prayers 48
Substance Abuse..48
Bondage vs. Freedom 50
Rebellion vs. Submission 51

PART III...53
Veterans' Curses..54
Prayer to Break Foreign Curses 56
What is PTSD..57
Prayer to Restore your Brain 62

PART IV 65
Spoken Word..66
Word Scriptures...76
Who You Are In Christ 77

Spiritual Authority 79

PART V **83**
Prayers:
Discouragement 84
Fear/Anxiety/Worry 86
Grief 89
Guilt/Shame 91
Harassing and Tormenting Spirits 93
Heaviness/Depression/Suicidal
Thoughts 95
Horrifying Thoughts and Dreams 97
Mental Strongholds 99
Oppression 101
Peace 103
Protection 105
Trust 108
Books and References Studied 110
Books by Little Sparrow Ministries 114

PART I
Beginning Prayer, Deception, Forgiveness, Root of Bitterness, Releasing Ungodly Soul-Ties, Prayer to Restore Fragmented Souls, Testimony

PLEASE PRAY OUT LOUD.

BEGINNING PRAYER

1 John 3:8 ...*The reason the Son of God appeared was to destroy the devil's work.*

Proverbs 11:21 ...*but those who are righteous will go free.*

Psalms 68:6 ...*He leads forth the prisoners with singing...*

Heavenly Father,

I ask you to destroy the works of the devil – his plans and schemes – in my life. You said in your word, *"Now the Lord is the Spirit: and where the Spirit of the Lord is, there is freedom."* (2 Corinthians 3:17) Have mercy on me. I am seeking you for complete freedom from the works of the Satan.

Now with the authority given to me by my Lord Jesus Christ, I speak to every evil spirit, and I demand that you are bound to silence. You cannot inflict any pain, speak to my mind, prevent me from hearing and seeing spiritual truths, or speaking truths. Amen.

PLEASE PRAY OUT LOUD.

DECEPTION

Psalms 12:2   *Everyone lies to his neighbor; their flattering lips speak with deception.*

Proverbs 26:26   *His malice may be concealed by deception, but his wickedness will be exposed in the assembly.*

Hosea 10:13   *But you have planted wickedness, you have reaped evil. You have eaten the fruit of deception, because you have depended on your own strength and on your many warriors...*

Jeremiah 9:6   *You live in the midst of deception; in their deceit they refuse to acknowledge me, declares the Lord.*

Proverbs 14:8   *The wisdom of the prudent is to give thought to their ways, but the folly of fools is deception.*

2 Corinthians 4:2   *Rather, we have renounced secret and shameful ways; we do not use deception, nor do we distort the word of God. On the contrary, by setting forth the truth plainly, we commend ourselves to every man's conscience in the sight of God.*

PLEASE PRAY OUT LOUD.

Heavenly Father,

We live in a world controlled by the evil one, but thankfully, we are not of this world. For the ungodly, deception has become a way of life; and they refuse to acknowledge you, Lord.

As your children, we live by your word. John 8:31-32 states, *"If you hold to my teaching, you are really my disciples. Then you will know the truth, and the truth will set you free."*

In the name of Jesus, I bind, break the soul-ties, break your power, and cast out of me the strongman of lying spirits, dormant spirits, familiar spirits, and familial spirits. I demand that you separate from me now. Go to the arid places, and never return. Holy Spirit please fill all void places within me.

Lord, I ask you to loosen truth and discernment. As darkness and deception no longer surrounds me, I now have the ability to see the truth, and will not be caught in the web of the enemy's lies. Amen.

SPIRIT OF OFFENSE

Forgiveness is truly at the heart of God. God sees us through his eyes of love. "Lord, please allow us to see through your eyes."

We cannot live in this world without becoming offended. So we must prepare for this deadly trap of Satan's – the spirit of offense. We do not want demonic strongholds in our lives. It would stop God's plans for us and our sensitivity to him.

Our lives are based on relationships. With spiritual laws and truths, the word of God shows each of us how to live Godly lives. God is concerned with our behavior. Does our behavior reflect his love, kindness, gentleness, compassion, and mercy?

In Matthew 24, one of the signs of his impending return is, *"many will be offended."* He will demand agape love from us – unconditional love.

Sometimes we may offend others knowingly or unknowingly. The reverse can also happen, and we can become offended or wronged. Then do we ACT with Godly wisdom or REACT in an ungodly manner.

There are three categories of wrongs or offenses:

1. Offenses you have committed.

    You must go immediately to the individual, and ask for forgiveness.

2. Offenses that have actually been committed against you.

3. Offenses that you have perceived have been committed against you, but actually were not.

A reaction to an offense can be hurt, disappointment, frustration, anger, and resentment.

Only those you care about can hurt you. You expect more from them. After all, you have given more of yourself to them. The more severe offenses are caused by close relationships. We expect these behaviors in the world and not in our churches. Many people in the church become wounded, hurt, and bitter.

When we become offended or wronged, the enemy will try to keep the offense hidden and surrounded in pride. Pride will keep you from admitting your true condition. Pride masks the true condition of your heart. It keeps you from dealing with the truth. It distorts your vision. Pride hardens your heart; and, as a result, you truly cannot see clearly.

You could begin to view yourself as a victim. You could hold back forgiveness, and you could create barriers or walls of protection around you so that no one else can hurt you. We become focused on ourselves and the injustices. This reduces or removes tenderness, and it creates a loss of sensitivity. We are then hindered in our ability to hear God's voice. This situation becomes a perfect scenario for the spirit of deception to operate.

Betrayal in a close relationship can be devastating. To betray someone is the ultimate abandonment of covenant. When betrayal occurs, the relationship cannot be restored unless genuine repentance follows. It happens all the time in our homes through divorce and splits in churches. We must come to the place where we trust God and not ourselves. The Key is to ACT – not react. The acts of forgiveness and release of the offense to the Lord are the first steps we must take.

I attended a meeting with a speaker from Ghana. His father was chief of a tribe and had many wives. One of his father's wives had his mother killed. From that day on, he and his brothers and sisters lived in poverty; they were outcasts from his father. As a young man, he gave his life to the Lord; and he became a preacher. He also thought he had forgiven his step-mother for killing his mother.

The Lord dealt with him on this matter. As a result, he approached his step-mother and told her that he forgave her. She immediately became emotional, and she asked him for forgiveness. She took Jesus in her heart, and she became saved. As a result of his obedience, all of the wives and most of the children were eventually saved; the whole tribe became Christians.

This testimony greatly affected me. Imagine, he forgave the person who killed his mother; and this man and his brothers and sisters lived their childhood in poverty because of their mother's death. In the past, it had been easier for me to forgive a person rather than to actually confront them. However, the word states:

Matthew 18:*15 If your brother sins against you, go and show him his fault, just between the two of you. If he listens to you, you have won your brother over.*

We resist the devil by not becoming offended. We must stay obedient to God. Do what He tells us to do. It may be to go to the individual and ask for forgiveness. It may be to do nothing more than pray for the individual. At a later time, He may have you do something – like write a letter.

However, if you have offended someone, ask the Holy Spirit to lead you. Most likely the Lord will tell you to go to them in love. Hold your tongue, and let them speak. In humility, ask them to forgive you if you have offended them in any way. You may not agree with what they have to say. Explain to them that you will ask the Holy Spirit to reveal all hidden truths.

On another occasion, a couple in my church spoke negatively of my ministry. I wanted to speak to them, but they refused any contact with me. I continually asked God what to do. I kept praying for them, and asking for all truths to come to the light.

Several months later during a church service, the Lord spoke to me. He said," Go the woman, and ask her if you have offended her. If so, ask her to forgive you." I said, "Lord, she will not speak to me." He said, "Haven't I told you to go to them seventy-seven times."

Matthew 18: 21-22 *Then Peter came to Jesus and asked, "Lord, how many times shall I forgive my brother when he sins against me? Up to seven times?" Jesus answered, "I tell you, not seven times, but seventy-seven times."*

Eventually the wife spoke to me, and said, "Judy, the problem is not you. It is my husband. He has baggage to deal with and refuses to see and hear the truth." You see I was working with one of his children who needed to be set free.

The enemy has tried to torment me with the hurts and wounds of the past, but I will not entertain those thoughts. I rebuke them, and I put them immediately out of my mind. It is past history, and I need to live in the present.

Philippians 4:8 *Finally, brothers, whatever is true, whatever is noble, whatever is right, whatever is pure, whatever is lovely, whatever is admirable-if anything is excellent or praiseworthy-think about such things.*

There are spiritual principles at work here. I asked for forgiveness, and received forgiveness from God. I forgave the other party, and was obedient to our Lord when He told me what to do. **The Keys are: forgiveness and obedience.** I asked for forgiveness; I gave forgiveness. I listened, and I obeyed the leading of the Holy Spirit.

Love is the tool that keeps us free from the lies and darts of the enemy. We must put on the Armor of God daily (Ephesians 6:12). The importance of the shoes of the gospel of peace must never be forgotten. We must walk in peace with our fellow man. However, we are never to compromise the truths of God in order to walk in that peace. Remember, the keys are forgiveness and obedience.

Colossians 3:12-14 *Therefore, as God's chosen people, holy and dearly loved, clothe yourselves with compassion, kindness, humility, gentleness and patience. Bear with each other and forgive whatever grievances you may have against one another. Forgive as the Lord forgave you. And over all these virtues put on love, which binds them all together in perfect unity.*

To forgive is a decision you must make. It has nothing to do with your emotions or "how you feel." By being willing to forgive, God will honor that decision; he will help you remove the unforgiveness, resentment, and bitterness. All it takes is your "will" to be obedient to God. Unforgiveness, resentment, and bitterness can cause physical illnesses, i.e. arthritis, aches, and pains in our body.

FORGIVENESS

2 Chronicles 7:14   *If my people who are called by my name will humble themselves, and pray and seek my face, and turn from their wicked ways, then I will hear from heaven, and will forgive their sin and heal their land.*

James 5:15   *And the prayer offered in faith will make the sick person well; the Lord will raise him up. If he has sinned, he will be forgiven.*

Luke 7:47   *Therefore, I tell you, her many sins have been forgiven – for she loved much. But he who is forgiven little loves little.*

Mark 11:25-26   *And when you stand praying, if you hold anything against anyone, forgive him, so that your Father in heaven may forgive you your sins.*

1 John 1:9   *If we confess our sins, he is faithful and just and will forgive us our sins and purify us from all unrighteousness.*

Psalms 86:5   *You are forgiving and good, O Lord, abounding in love to all who call to you.*

PLEASE PRAY OUT LOUD.

Heavenly Father,

Forgive me for harboring any unforgiveness, resentment, and bitterness. Please reveal to my mind those that I have offended or need to forgive. Help me, Holy Spirit, to stay obedient to our Lord. Convict me of all my wrong doings so that I may walk closer to the light. Amen.

Please pray for those whom you have offended or need to forgive.

Lord, forgive me for whatever I have done to _____ (name of person).

Lord, forgive _____ (name of person) for whatever they have done to me.

Lord, I forgive _____ (name of person).

Lord, forgive us for what we have both done to you.

I release _____ (name of person).

ROOT OF BITTERNESS

Hebrew 12:15 *See to it that no one comes short of the grace of God; that no root of bitterness springing up causes trouble, and by it many be defiled.*

Definition: Bitterness can be defined as profound grief, anguish, or disappointment accompanied by suppressed hostility towards unbearable circumstances. Difficult to accept, admit, or bear. Marked by resentment, cynicism, emotional pain, and anger.

Cause: It almost always begins by your becoming offended. Someone says something or does something so that your feelings are hurt, and you become offended. Then, at the moment you become offended, we see the enemy start his war. The battleground is your mind; he tries to push you beyond offended, into being angry and bitter. Many times our pride has been wounded.

The enemy tries, according to John 10:10, *"to kill, steal, and destroy"* our lives and to create spiritual barriers between you and the Lord. Rick Joyner of Morningstar Ministries states, "That by maintaining these things in our lives, we are actually being a better host to the devil than we are to the Spirit."

Manifestations of the Root of Bitterness:

- **Physical Illnesses**: There can be a link between what we think and the way our bodies function. Bitterness, anger, and other negative emotions can be associated with glandular problems, high blood pressure, cardiac disorders, ulcers, and other physical ailments.

- **Broken/Strained Relationships**: The bitterness we nourish will strain our relationships. The roots of bitterness, anger, resentment, and hatred that we carry can build barriers that prevent us from loving our spouses and children. This is one reason why there are so many separations, divorces, and broken homes. Our ungodly behavior affects all those around us.

- **Barriers between You and God**: Unforgiveness can hinder your faith and prevent your prayers from being answered. It can stop your harvest.

Mark 11:25 *And when you stand praying, if you hold anything against anyone, forgive him, so that your Father in heaven may forgive you your sins.*

Getting Rid of Bitterness:

1. Ask the Lord to show you how you developed the root of bitterness, the individual involved, and the offense. Was it actually an offense against you or was it a perceived offense?

2. If you have stuffed your feelings concerning this offense, allow the Lord to bring them to the surface.

3. Thank God for this offense because He will use this offense to conform you into his image and to bring glory to him.

4. Pray the **Forgiveness Prayer** on page 13 and ask God to remove all bitterness, anger, resentment, and hatred. Also, forgive yourself.

5. Ask God to help you view the person who has wronged you as a tool in the hands of God.

6. Know that Jesus is always holding out his arms of forgiveness and love. He cannot even remember the unforgiveness and bitterness that was keeping you in bondage.

7. If you feel it is appropriate, go to the person, confess your bitterness and ask for forgiveness. **Remember**

you are assuming the responsibility for your attitude; you are not trying to solicit repentance.

Matthew 18:15-20 says, *"If your brother sins against you, go and show him his fault, just between the two of you. If then he listens to you, you have won your brother over. But if he will not listen, take one or two others along with you, so that every matter may be established by two or three witnesses. If he refuses to listen to them, tell it to the church; and if he refuses to listen even to the church, treat him as you would a pagan or a tax collector. I tell you the truth, whatever you bind on earth will be bound in heaven, and whatever you loose on earth is loosed in heaven. Again, I tell you that if two of you on earth agree about anything you ask for, it will be done for you by my Father in heaven. For where two or three come together in my name, there am I with them."*

Ok, you have started. Let us dig a little deeper. You still have the list of people that have wounded you. Add to that list events, accidents, abuse, military service, etc. that have contributed to you developing PTSD. Take your time, and ask God to bring events to your memory so that you can write them down.

After you have developed your list, find a quiet place with no distractions. I went into a church and stayed there all day. Take a large quantity of paper with you and a couple of pens or pencils. Also, take water and some tissues with you.

1. Pray for God's help.

2. Start to write letters to people who have wounded you. These letters are all about why you are angry. Remember to include God and yourself. GET THE POISON OUT. Get angry and put it all down on paper. If you have been in the military, write letters to the president or the officers over you. (Oh, by the way, you will not mail them.)

If you have been abused, you must forgive. We will deal with the issues involved in this situation a little later. If tragic deaths have contributed to your trauma, write letters to all involved including God and your family members or friends who are deceased.

This is going to take you quite a while. Do not hurry! Take your time. Get it all out. **This is a very important step in your recovery.**

3. Now write letters to each person forgiving them of their actions including God and especially yourself. Take your time. Ask God to change your heart and your emotions regarding these situations.

After you have completed all assignments, go to a Christian counselor, pastor, or even a Christian friend. Begin reading out loud the angry letters. Next, read your forgiveness letters.

The next step is to pray the ungodly soul-ties prayer and the fragmentation of your soul prayer. Both prayers are next. Your soul has been fragmented (broken) over all of your wounding. You now need your soul restored.

At the end of this section, there is a testimony of my recovery from PTSD. Please read it; I pray it will help you.

RELEASING UNGODLY SOUL-TIES PRAYER

Genesis 2:24 *For this reason a man will leave his father and mother and be united to his wife, and they will become one flesh.*

1 Samuel 14:7 *"Do all that you have in mind," his armor-bearer said. "Go ahead; I am with you heart and soul."*

Man is divided into three distinct parts: body, soul, and spirit. **Spirit:** When we are born again, our spirit is divinely connected with the Holy Spirit. The Holy Spirit resides within us. **Soul:** Our soul is composed of our mind (intellect), will, and emotions. **Body:** Our body (flesh) houses our spirit and soul.

A soul-tie can be described as the linking together of two individuals, i.e. becoming one in their souls. God designed a soul-tie as a two-way interaction for the flow of love between two parties.

Soul-ties can become ungodly and harmful. According to Bill and Sue Banks, in ***Breaking Unhealthy Soul-Ties,*** "Soul-ties can either be intellectual, emotional, or erotic.

- "Intellectual or platonic soul-ties such as between a student – teacher can become ungodly if it turns into dependence, bondage, or idolatry.

- "Emotional soul-ties between a husband and wife, children, parents, step-family, and other family members can be based on feelings of love, hatred, or fear. It can also become ungodly as a result of adultery, manipulation, control, or co-dependency.

- "An erotic soul-tie is a physical soul-tie formed as a result of sin."

It is possible that a soul-tie can develop to an addiction (idolatry). If that idolatry has consumed a person's body, soul, and spirit, an ungodly link has occurred with that addiction.

To break ungodly soul-ties, please pray the following:

PLEASE PRAY OUT LOUD.

In the name of Jesus, I break the ungodly soul-tie with _____ (name or substance).

Lord, I ask that you cleanse me from all unrighteousness as a result of any known or unknown agreement that resulted in an ungodly soul-tie. I ask that you sever all strongholds that have formed as a result of this ungodly action. Forgive me, Lord, for my part in creating this ungodly soul-tie. Amen.

Also break the soul-tie with the deceased, divorced, or abandoned spouse; and break the soul-ties with deceased friends or family. After breaking the soul-ties, please pray the fragmentation prayer.

PLEASE PRAY OUT LOUD.

FRAGMENTATION OF OUR SOUL PRAYER

Most everyone has been wounded by others, abused, and grieved over a loss. Some handle tragic events better than others. However, most of us have a difficult time recovering from the wounding. Because of this intensive wounding, our soul can become fragmented. You might say it breaks into small parts. Sometimes the enemy can become attached to these parts, and it can make our lives miserable.

To totally recover from this fragmentation, we must:

1. Forgive

2. Break soul-ties

3. Repent from any and all sins

When you feel you have done all you can do, then pray the following prayer – out loud:

Lord Jesus, I come to you as a wounded child. My heart feels as if it is broken into a million pieces. I need you to restore my body, soul, and spirit.

I ask you, Lord, to heal all the fragmented pieces of my soul. If there are any demonic spirits attached to the pieces, I demand, in Jesus name, that you leave and get out of my soul now. You no longer have any legal right to stay.

I ask you, Lord, to put all the pieces together and restore my soul. I declare that because my soul is restored my body and spirit are also restored. Thank you Lord. Amen.

TESTIMONY OF JUDY H. FARRIS-SMITH

I have been healed of this syndrome by my Lord and Savior, Jesus Christ. I can only tell you how he healed me. I know that our Lord is not a respecter of persons; if he did it for me, he will do it for you.

I met my first husband when I was about 12 years of age. When I started attending middle school, I saw this young man in the cafeteria line. I did not know his name or anything about him. I knew that one day we would be married, and that God had chosen him as my soul-mate.

Throughout our school years, we were thrown together and started dating. After I graduated from high school, my family moved to Florida from Illinois. Our relationship weakened for several years. However, the Lord brought us back together, and eventually we were married. So you can see my husband and I had a strong soul-tie. We were married for twenty-six years, when suddenly he died of cancer. He died almost overnight.

When this happened so quickly, my mind went into shock. I had no family around except my sixteen year old son. He was dealing with his grief in his own way, and he had very little communication with me. I remember watching a blank TV screen for hours on end. People stopped calling me, and I was left alone. This lasted for approximately six months.

I knew I was in a spiritual battle. I could feel the enemy in my mind telling me one thing after another. I held onto the Bible with all my might, and even slept with it. I could not understand what was happening to me.

God, through a divine appointment, paired me with a Christian counselor who was also a deliverance minister. I remember she told me that she was not sure if she could help me. I did not know what she meant. I did not know that my pupils were fixed. I only knew that people kept looking into my eyes, and I could not understand why.

During our counseling sessions, my counselor kept asking me if I had forgiven everyone. "Of course," I said. One day in church on a Sunday morning, I heard the audible voice of God say, "Forgive him." I asked the person sitting next to me if she heard that voice. She said, "Yes, I heard the pastor." I was tormented, and I could not understand what was going on with me.

By Tuesday morning, I was so tormented that I called the counselor, and I told her I was coming to see her. She then instructed me to do the following:

1. I was sent to the church where I started writing letters to everyone in my life who had harmed or wounded me. I was verbally and physically abused (beaten) as a child so this activity took quite awhile. In fact, I sat in the church and wrote letters for about eight hours. By the way, the letters were not to be sent to anyone. They were just meant to unload and to forgive.

2. The first letters were for me to release the poison that had accumulated within me. Everything that had happened to me my entire life was being exposed as I wrote the truth as I saw it. They were angry and tormented letters. I wrote letters also to God and myself. I was angry because God had let my husband die. I was angry with my deceased husband because he had died, and he left me alone.

3. The second set of letters was forgiveness letters. I had let the anger, hurt, and resentment come forth in the first set of letters. My heart began to soften. I felt the love of the Lord come into my body, soul, and spirit. I could now forgive. I painstakingly wrote letters to everyone who had harmed me. I could feel a release within my body, soul, and spirit.

4.   After I finished with the letters, I went back to the counselor's office where I read each and every letter to her and a pastor at the church. As I read them out loud, I could feel the love of the Lord. His love for me was so strong that it was overwhelming.

I then left her office and went home. I knew I had done what God had wanted me to do. I rested.

Being in shock, I was unable to perform my work related duties efficiently. I was doing accounting work, and it took me twice as long to complete my work. So often I would go back to the office in the late afternoon or evening. One day, not long after the experience in the counselor's office, I went back to the office to finish some work. I heard a knock at the office door. It was the maintenance man, and he came into the office to check on me. All of a sudden, I was furious because he was checking on me. I was extremely angry, but something happened at that moment. I could feel a shift in my brain; I could feel a change.

God is so good. After that experience and within about three or four weeks, I was almost back to normal. I was still a little paranoid, but had clear thinking and was starting to enjoy life again.

If He can do this for me, He can do this for you. All things are possible with God. I know that miracles have happened to me, and they can happen to you. I know He loves me, protects me, and directs me.

If you are experiencing traumatic shock, perhaps the above steps will help you in overcoming this difficult time in your life. <u>You will be whole again!</u>

PART II

Generational Curses, Prayers for Breaking Generational Curses, Occult Practices Inventory, Occult Practices Prayer, Substance Abuse, Bondage vs. Freedom, Rebellion vs. Submission

GENERATIONAL CURSES

My people perish from lack of knowledge. Hosea 4:6

Curse n. A prayer or invocation for harm or injury to come upon one; evil or misfortune that comes as if in response to imprecation or as a retribution; a cause of great harm or misfortune.

Curse v. To use profanely insolent language against, blaspheme; to call upon divine or supernatural power to send injury upon; to execrate in fervent and often profane terms; to bring great evil upon, afflict. *(Merriam-Webster's Collegiate Dictionary 1994, 1995)*

Does your family have continuous problems with: poverty, barrenness, depression, anger, sicknesses such as cancer, and heart disease, rebellion, catastrophic accidents, mental illness, suicides, addictions, divorce, abuse, sexual sins? The list could go on and on.

Are you a Christian that attends church regularly and does everything possible to lead a godly life and are still plagued by the above problems and more? The answer could be curses that have been allowed on your family line because of:

1. Generational sins

2. Involvement in the occult
3. Negative spoken words
4. Personal sins which open doors
5. Ungodly soul ties from other individuals and groups

As a result of the above, curses may have been allowed on your ancestors, you, and your family by:

- God
- Satan having a legal right to curse
- Satan and demonic spirits that do not have a legal right to curse

1. Generational Curses

Research your family's history and determine if the same problems are passed down from one generation to the next; that is called a generational curse. Can you see a pattern? **Through conception, weaknesses and behavioral tendencies are passed down to us as a result of inheriting the iniquities of our fathers.** Thereby, the curses are passed on to each successive generation as they commit the same sins.

Lamentations 5:7 *Our fathers sinned and are no more, and we bear their punishment.*

Numbers 14:18 *The Lord is slow to anger, abounding in love and forgiving sin and rebellion. Yet He does not leave the guilty unpunished; He punishes the children for the sins of the fathers to the third and fourth generations.*

Jeremiah 15:13 *Your wealth and your treasures I will give as plunder, without charge, because of all your sins throughout your country.*

Jeremiah 6:19 *Hear, O earth: I am bringing disaster on this people, the fruit of their schemes, because they have not listened to my words and have rejected my law.*

We are responsible for our own actions and lack of knowledge does not excuse us from knowing the truth. God still holds us accountable. Therefore, we must read and understand God's word.

Leviticus 5:17 *If a person sins and does what is forbidden in any of the Lord's commands, even though he does not know it, he is guilty and will be held responsible.*

The key to preventing generational curses is consistent repentance for our sins, known and unknown. We must ask God to cleanse us, set us free, and change our behavior. The Holy Spirit will direct and guide us, if we only ask him.

Isaiah 5:13-14   *Therefore my people will go into exile for lack of understanding; their men of rank will die of hunger and their masses will be parched with thirst. Therefore, the grave enlarges its appetite and opens its mouth without limit; into it will descend their nobles and masses with all their brawlers and revelers.*

2. Involvement in the occult

Curses can be derived from your involvement in the occult or from other people that have been under Satan's authority.

3. Negative spoken words

We must carefully scrutinize our vocabulary. *"For by your words you will be acquitted, and by your words you will be condemned."* (Matthew 12:37)

4. Personal sins

The key is consistent repentance for your sins and living according to God's truths.

5.   Ungodly soul-ties

Be aware of soul-ties of the past and the soul-ties that are created by you in the future.

- Curses allowed by God

In the seventh chapter of Joshua, Israel sinned against God and as a result thirty-six of its men perished.

Joshua 7:1 *But the Israelites acted unfaithfully in regard to the devoted things; Achan son of Carmi, the son of Zimri, the son of Zerah, of the tribe of Judah, took some of them. So the Lord's anger burned against Israel.*

The children of Israel were cursed by God many times as a result of their unrepentant sins and disobedience.

- Curses placed by Satan who has a legal right.

If we knowingly or unknowingly have sinned, we can cause a door to open for Satan and his demonic spirits legally to enter. God does not destroy or bring calamity upon us, but he does allow Satan at times to do so.

- Curses placed by Satan who does not have a legal right.

Because we are Christians who are walking righteously with the Lord, Satan will send tormenting spirits in various forms to harass, discourage, defile, deceive, compel, enslave, and to cause fear, and sickness. God has given us the power and authority to bind the strongmen and their demonic spirits, and we are to rebuke their actions.

PLEASE PRAY OUT LOUD.

PRAYERS FOR BREAKING GENERATIONAL CURSES

Ask the Holy Spirit to show you what curses have been placed on you and your ancestors. To break curses allowed by God, Satan who has a legal right, and Satan, who does not have a legal right, please pray the following prayers in the order indicated:

1. Prayer for breaking curses allowed by God.

Heavenly Father, I come to you in the name of our Lord Jesus Christ and by virtue of his shed blood. I ask you to forgive me of my sins and the sins of my forefathers, those that are known and are not known. Lord, I ask that you remove and completely destroy all the roots and seeds of my own personal sins and my ancestors' sins. I ask you to separate me from the generational curse or curses that you have allowed on my life as a result of the sins of my forefathers or my own personal sins. I ask you to shut the blood line doors that were opened as a result of my own personal sins and my ancestors' sins. Thank you, Lord. Amen.

2. Prayers for breaking curses from Satan having legal authority.

By the authority and power given to me by the holy name of our Lord, Jesus Christ, I bind, break the soul-ties, break your power, and cast off of me the strongmen of: the spirit of divination, familiar spirit, spirit of jealousy, lying spirit, perverse spirit, spirit of haughtiness, spirit of heaviness, spirit of whoredoms, spirit of infirmity, dumb and deaf spirit, spirit of bondage, spirit of fear, seducing spirits, spirit of anti-Christ, spirit of error, and spirit of death and all other demonic spirits that were associated with any and all generational curses which include familiar spirits, familial spirits, and dormant spirits. I demand that you separate from me now as you have no legal right to stay. I ask you to shut the blood line doors that were opened as a result of my own personal sins and my ancestors' sins. Go to the arid places, and never return. Holy Spirit please come and fill the void places within me. Amen.

3. In the next prayer as you take the authority given to you by our Lord, Jesus Christ, please insert the names of any demonic spirits that have tormented and harassed you and your ancestors. A few examples are cancer, arthritis, divorce, abortion, poverty, anger, offense, rejection, and negative thoughts.

By the authority and power given to me by the holy name of our Lord, Jesus Christ, I demand this curse of _____ (e.g. poverty, cancer, anger, suicide) to be broken now and forever more. I bind, break the soul-ties, break your power, and cast out of me all demonic spirits, familiar spirits, familial spirits, and dormant spirits that were associated with this curse. I demand you to separate from me now as you have no legal right to stay. I ask you to shut the blood line doors that were opened as a result of my own personal sins and my ancestors' sins. Go to the arid places, and never return. Holy Spirit please come and fill the void places within me. Amen.

Other wrongful behaviors may have gained a stronghold in your life. It could be due to your sin or the sins of your ancestors. No matter what the reason, you now have the tools to break these curses and change your behavior. To prevent future ancestral curses, **you must repent if you have sinned.** You must change your behavior, and walk in truth and righteousness.

OCCULT PRACTICES INVENTORY

The following is a list of cults, cultic religions, and occult activities that you may have been involved in. This list is not all-inclusive.

Cults and Religions

A Course in Miracles
Buddhism
Children of God
Christian Science
Earth Liberation
Eckankar
Freemasonry
Hare Krishna
Heaven's Gate
Hinduism
Indian Gurus
International Church of Christ (ICOC)
Islam
Jehovah's Witnesses
Mormonism/Latter-Day Saints
New Age Movement
Roman Catholicism
Rosicrucian
Satanism
Science of Mind
Scientology
Silva Mind Control
Taoism
Theosophical Society
Unification Church
Unitarianism
Unity Church
Way International

Occult Activities

Acupuncture, Alchemy
Altered states of consciousness, Animism,
Aquarian age, Aromatherapy, Ascended masters,
Astral projection, Astrology, Attitudinal healing,
Aura, Automatic writing,
Biofeedback, Blood pacts,
Centering, Chakras, Channeling,
Clairvoyance, Crystals, Dream catchers,
Dream therapy, Earth temples, Encounter groups,
Goddess worship, Guided imagery,
Hand writing analysis, Horoscopes,
Human potential movement, Hypnosis,
Iridology, Ikebana flower arranging, Levitation,
Magic, Magnetic therapy, Mandalas, Mantras,
Martial arts, Meditation, Necromancy,
New Age subliminal programming,
New Age music and heavy metal music,
Numerology, Occult literature and pictures,
Occult games i.e. Dungeon and Dragons,
Ouija Board, Out-of-body experiences,
Palm reading, Parapsychology, Pendulums,
Pokémon, Progressive relaxation, Pyramid power,
Reiki, Rod, Pendulum, Dowsing,
Séances, Self-esteem education, Self-realization,
Shaman, Sorcery Tarot cards, Tai Chi, Tattooing,
Tea leaf reading, Transpersonal education,
Telepathy, Visualization, Voodoo,
Witchcraft, Wicca, Yin & Yang, Yoga, and Zen sand gardens.

Also include initiation rites and involvement in lodges, brotherhoods, sororities, fraternities, honor societies, clubs, and shrines that would require an oath to uphold man-made doctrine (contrary to Christianity).

PLEASE PRAY OUT LOUD.

OCCULT PRACTICES PRAYER

Deuteronomy 18: 10-13 *Let no one be found among you who sacrifices his son or daughter in the fire, who practices divination or sorcery, interprets omens, engages in witchcraft, or casts spells, or who is a medium or spiritist, or who consults the dead. Anyone who does these things is detestable to the Lord, and because of these detestable practices the Lord your God will drive out those nations before you. You must be blameless before the Lord your God.*

Leviticus 19:26 *...Do not practice divination or sorcery.*

Leviticus 19:31 *Do not turn to mediums or seek out spiritists, for you will be defiled by them.*

PLEASE PRAY OUT LOUD.

Heavenly Father, I ask you to reveal to my mind the truth. Lord, reveal to me all my involvements with occult practices - either knowingly or unknowingly; reveal all occult deceptions that I have allowed in my life. Amen.

Write down everything God brings to your mind. (Use the Occult Practices Inventory.) Be sure to include oaths or initiation rites in which you have been a participant.

Using your list, <u>pray out loud</u> the following:

In the name of Jesus, I confess that I have participated in _____, (list all) and I ask you to forgive me for my involvement in these sins. I ask you, Lord, to cut the soul-tie with Satan and destroy or cancel any contract with Satan. Please give me the discernment to see the truth and not be caught in the web of Satan's lies.

In the name of Jesus, I bind, break the soul-ties, break your power, and cast off of me: the strongmen of divination, familiar spirits, demonic spirits, hidden and dormant spirits, and familial spirits. I demand that you leave me now as you have no legal right to stay. Go to the arid places and never return. I demand that my occult blood line doors are shut. Holy Spirit come and fill the void places within me. Amen.

If you have been involved in secretive organizations, pray: Lord, I renounce the oaths taken, the curses, the penalties, and its secretive passwords involved with _____ (name of organization).

If you have Indian ancestors, pray:

In the name of Jesus, I renounce all the lies, deceptions, practices, rituals, idols, and sacrifices that are part of the Indian culture. I ask for forgiveness for my ignorance and actions. In the name of Jesus, I bind, break the soul-ties, break your power, and cast out of me: the spirit of victimization, medicine man spirit, demonic spirits, hidden and dormant spirits, familiar spirits, and familial spirits that are associated with the Indian life style.

In the name of Jesus, I renounce and break the power of Indian witchcraft. I demand that the curses from my Indian blood lines are broken and shattered, and I am separated from them. I demand that the doors that were opened due to curses from my Indian blood line are shut. I demand you leave me now as you have no legal right to stay. Go to the arid places, and never return. Holy Spirit come and fill the void places within me. Amen.

If you have Aztec and/or Mayan ancestors, please pray the following:

In the name of Jesus, I renounce all the lies, deceptions, practices, rituals, idols, and blood sacrifices that were a part of the Aztec and/or Mayan cultures. In the name of Jesus, I bind, break the soul-ties, break your power, and cast out of me: the spirit of witchcraft, occult, familiar spirits, familial spirits, hidden and dormant spirits, demonic spirits, and any other strongmen associated with the Aztec and/or Mayan cultures.

I demand that the doors that were opened from the curses from my Aztec and/or Mayan blood lines are shut. I am separated from them. I demand you leave me now as you have no legal right to stay. Go to the arid places, and never return. Holy Spirit come and fill the void places within me. Amen.

Gypsies: A member of a nomadic Caucasoid people with dark skin and black hair, found throughout the world and believed to have originated in India: they are conventionally known as metalworkers, musicians, fortune-tellers, etc. (Syn: Romany, Rommany, Romani, Roma, Bohemian, Sinti, Dom, Lyuli, Banjara, Domba, Irish Travelers, Scottish Highland Travelers, Yeniche, Sea Gypsies) (*Wikipedia 2011*) One of a vagabond race, whose tribes, coming originally from India, entered Europe in the 14th or 15th century, and are now scattered over Turkey, Russia, Hungary, Spain, England, etc., living by theft, fortune-telling, horse jockeying, tinkering, etc. (*Webster's Dictionary*)

If you have been a gypsy or have gypsy ancestors, please pray the following:

In the name of Jesus, I renounce all the lies, deceptions, practices, rituals, and idols that are a part of the gypsy culture. I ask for forgiveness for my ignorance and ungodly actions. In the name of Jesus, I bind, break the soul-ties, break your power, and cast off of me: the strongmen of divination and familiar spirits, occult, familial spirits, hidden and dormant spirits, and demonic spirits associated with the gypsy culture.

I demand that the doors that were opened from the curses from my gypsy blood lines are shut. I am separated from them. I demand you leave me now as you have no legal right to stay. Go to arid places, and never return. Holy Spirit come and fill the void places within me. Amen.

PLEASE PRAY OUT LOUD.

ADDITIONAL DELIVERANCE PRAYERS

SUBSTANCE ABUSE

Lord, I repent for loving the sin of _____ (e.g. alcohol, food, drugs, and prostitutes), and I repent for loving this sin more than you. Please forgive me. Please remove the love for this sin and cause me to love you more. Change my body, mind-set, and brain functions to reflect the absence of this sin in my life.

Lord, I ask that you remove and completely destroy all the roots and seeds of my sins of substance abuse and ungodly sex, and my ancestors' sins of substance abuse and ungodly sex. Consider any satanic pact made by me or my ancestors null and void. Lord, I ask you to separate me from all generational curses which have resulted in my addiction, ungodly sex, and substance abuse. I also shut all blood line doors that were opened as a result of substance abuse, ungodly sex, and especially _____.

I confess that I have misused substances (e.g. alcohol, tobacco, food, prescriptions, street drugs, and ungodly sex) for the purpose of pleasure, to escape reality, or to cope with difficult situations resulting in the abuse of my body, the harmful programming of my mind, and the quenching of the Holy Spirit. I ask your forgiveness, and I renounce any satanic connection or influence in my life through my misuse of chemicals, sex, or food. Lord, I ask you to break the soul-ties with the substances and the participants in ungodly sex.

In the name of Jesus, I bind, break the soul-ties, break your power, and cast off of me: the strongmen of bondage, perversion, familiar spirit, spirit of addiction, all hidden and dormant spirits, familiar spirits, and familial spirits. I demand you to leave me now as you have no legal right to stay. I demand you to go to the arid places, and never return. You cannot attach yourself to me or anyone else. Holy Spirit please come and fill the void places within me.

I cast my anxieties onto Christ who loves me, and I commit myself to no longer yield to substance abuse and to ungodly sex but to the Holy Spirit. Amen.

PLEASE PRAY OUT LOUD.

BONDAGE vs. FREEDOM

Lord, you have told us to *"Cloth ourselves with the Lord Jesus Christ, and do not think about how to gratify the desires of the sinful nature."* (Romans 13:14) I acknowledge that I have not abstained from *"sinful desires, which wage war against my soul."* (1 Peter 2:11) I thank you that in Christ my sins are forgiven, and I am *"alive to God in Christ Jesus."* (Romans 6:11) I come before you to acknowledge these sins and to seek your cleansing so that I may be freed from the bondage of sin.

Lord, I ask you to forgive me of my sins and my ancestors' sins; those that are known or unknown. Lord, I ask that you remove and completely destroy all the roots and seeds of my sins and my ancestors' sins of bondage. Consider any satanic pact made by me or my ancestors null and void. Lord, I ask you to separate me from all generational curses which have resulted in bondage. I also shut all blood line doors that were opened as a result of the spirit of bondage. In the name of Jesus, I break all soul-ties that have been created while I have been in bondage.

In the name of Jesus, I bind, break soul-ties, break your power, and cast off of me: the strongman of bondage, hidden and dormant spirits, familiar spirits, and familial spirits. I demand you to leave me now as you have no legal right to stay. I demand you to go to the arid places, and never return. You cannot attach yourself to me or anyone else. Holy Spirit please come and fill the void places within me. Amen.

REBELLION vs. SUBMISSION

Lord, you have said that *"rebellion is as the sin of divination and arrogance like the evil of idolatry."* (1 Samuel 15:23) I know that in action and attitude I have sinned against you with a rebellious heart. I ask your forgiveness for my rebellion. I pray that by the shed blood of the Lord Jesus Christ that all ground gained by evil spirits because of my rebelliousness would be canceled. I pray that you will shed light on all my evil ways so that I may know the full extent of my rebelliousness.

Lord, I ask that you remove and completely destroy all the roots and seeds of my rebellious sins and my ancestors' rebellious sins. Consider any satanic pact made by me or my ancestors null and void. Lord, I ask you to separate me from all generational curses which have resulted in my rebelliousness. I also shut all blood line doors that were opened as a result of the spirit of rebellion. In the name of Jesus, I break all soul-ties that have been created with others while I committed this sinful activity.

I choose to adopt a submissive spirit and a servant's heart. I bind, break soul-ties, break your power, and cast off of me: the strongmen of lying spirits and divination, spirit of rebellion, and his demonic associates which include but not limited to hidden and dormant spirits, familiar spirits, and familial spirits. I demand you to leave me now as you have no legal right to stay. I demand you to go to the arid places, and never return. You cannot attach yourself to me or anyone else. Holy Spirit please come and fill the void places within me. Amen.

PART III

Veterans' Curses, Prayer to Break Foreign Curses, What is PTSD?, Prayer to Restore Your Brain

VETERANS' CURSES

We want to personally thank all veterans in all wars for your service to our country. We bless you beyond measure.

Veterans who have served in Iraq, Iran, Kuwait, Afghanistan, and other Middle Eastern countries need to know that Muslims, at their daily prayers, are cursing our veterans several times a day. Again our soldiers are battling spiritually as well as physically. The curses can take affect while they are in the foreign countries or when they get home. The soldiers will pick up spirits and they will come home with them. Again, we are dealing with spiritual warfare. The government tries to heal PTSD in the natural and mainly through medicines.

Our soldiers' only hope is through our Lord and Savior, Jesus Christ. When God is taken out of the picture by our government, our men and women are left without spiritual covering. I believe that most of our Christian soldiers do not have an understanding of spiritual warfare. Therefore, most of them are left with the effects of the satanic curses.

The following is a list of possible curses: death, poverty, confusion, hatred, anger, mental torment, spirit of suicide, insanity, misery, guilt, emotional hardness, antagonism, rejection, disgrace, shame, nightmares, drugs, prostitution, perversion, depression, amnesia, wandering or vagabond spirit, unbelief, rebellion, strife and division in families, divorce, dismemberment of bodies, crippling of bodies, blindness, hearing loss, calamities, and disease.

In Vietnam, Laos, Cambodia, and Thailand battles between tribes have continued for centuries. The religions in these areas were mainly Buddhism and Hinduism mixed with witchcraft. These areas have been given over to pagan spiritual powers. The Buddhist monks and other religious hierarchies prayed to their false gods, principalities, powers and rulers of darkness. When our men were in those countries, they fought on unholy ground and not only went into battle physically but spiritually as well.

Vietnamese Buddhist monks spent years heaping specific curses upon all Americans that came to fight in their countries. Some of these curses are:

- That they would be angry men and women all of their lives.
- That they would have a wandering spirit attached to them.
- That they would never find rest or peace.

PRAYER FOR BREAKING FOREIGN CURSES

In the name of Jesus, I bind and break all demonic powers of witchcraft. I break all word curses from demonic prayers originating from Buddhism, Islam, and Hinduism that have resulted in curses being placed on me and my family. I decree that these curses are broken on me and my family.

Lord, I have repented of all sins, known or unknown. I have shut all the blood line doors that were opened as the result of generational curses.

In the name of Jesus, I break the power of every evil word that was knowingly or unknowingly spoken against me by any person, cult, or group. I also break the power of any spoken curse that came out of my mouth.

In the name of Jesus, I now seal up the powers of everyone who spoke a curse over me and my family so that they cannot use them on anyone, and that their works might be destroyed, in the hope that their souls might be saved for the glory of God. Amen.

WHAT IS POST-TRAUMATIC STRESS DISORDER?

According to the National Institute of Mental Health:

"Post-Traumatic Stress Disorder, PTSD, is an anxiety disorder that can develop after exposure to a terrifying event or ordeal in which grave physical harm occurred or was threatened. Traumatic events that may trigger PTSD include violent personal assaults, natural or human-caused disasters, accidents, or military combat." (NIMH, 2009)

PTSD and Brain Chemistry

"Parts of the brain most involved in PTSD:

- Amygdala
- Hippocampus
- Medial front cortex
- Thalamus
- Hypothalamus
- Hypothalamic-pituitary-adrenal axis.

"Along with these, chemicals in the brain such as:

- Noradrenalin
- Dopamine
- Serotonin
- The opiod systems, insulin, and Cortisol all play complex roles in the PTSD symptom producing process." (Briere, 2009)

"The wiring of the brain's neurochemical systems becomes over sensitized. Resulting in the symptoms seen in PTSD. The complex chemical-neurological reactivity affects parts of the brain that are all about learning, memory, and fear conditioning." (Briere, 2009)

A neurochemical that plays a role in chronic stress is Cortisol.

"Cortisol is a hormone that is produced in the adrenal gland producing adrenaline. Also called the "stress hormone" because it tends to increase blood pressure, blood sugar levels, and has an immunosuppressive effect." (Briere, 2009).

"Secretion of Cortisol is prolonged during chronic stress or a traumatic event. This begins a vicious cycle of symptoms.

- Cortisol levels highest in the morning, lowest a few hours after sleep begins in the average person.
- This helps explain why many individuals who suffer from PTSD have disturbed sleep and nightmares.

"The most significant neurological impact of trauma is seen in the Hippocampus. Research has also suggested that the hippocampus may shrink and kill neurons.

- This may slow down the growth of new neurons.
- This has lead to understanding why individuals with PTSD have a hard time concentrating or remembering things.

Part of Brain	Normal Memory Function	Dysfunction due to stress
Hippocampus (sensitive to Cortisol)	Catalogs, stores, and retrieves normal memory.	Decreased ability to form new memories. Fragmented memory recall. Enhanced traumatic memories.
Amygdala (sensitive to noradrenalin)	Emotional memory, fear conditioning	Increased fear and sensitivity to fearful stimuli. Increased reactions to triggers. Enhanced traumatic memories.
Medial Prefrontal Cortex (improves with small increases in noradrenalin, blocked by large increases in noradrenalin)	Inhibition of irrelevant stimuli. Working memory. Inhibition of amygdale. Sustained attention.	Can't inhibit irrelevant stimuli. Decreased working memory. Can't inhibit emotions. Increased intrusive thoughts and memories. Decreased attention and concentration.

"Throughout the brain several chemical and biological imbalances can be present after trauma. Their effects are especially exacerbated by three major brain function dysregulations:

- **Over stimulated amygdala:** An almond-shaped mass located deep in the brain, the amygdala is responsible for survival-related threat identification, plus tagging memories with emotion. After trauma, the amygdala can get caught up in a highly alert and activated loop during which it looks for and perceives threat everywhere.

- **Underactive hippocampus:** An increase in the stress hormone glucocorticoid kills cells in the hippocampus, which renders it less effective in making synaptic connections necessary for memory consolidation. This interruption keeps both the body and mind stimulated in reactive mode as neither element receives the message that the threat has transformed into the past tense.

- **Ineffective variability:** The constant elevation of stress hormones interferes with the body's ability to regulate itself. The sympathetic nervous system remains highly activated leading to fatigue of the body and many of its systems, most notably the adrenal.

"While changes to the brain can seem, on the surface, disastrous and representative of permanent damage, the truth is that all of these alterations can be reversed. The amygdala can learn to relax; the hippocampus can resume proper memory consolidation; the nervous system can recommence its easy flow between reactive and restorative modes. The key to achieving a state of neutrality and then healing lies in helping to reprogram the body and mind." **Psychcentral.com**

PRAYER TO RESTORE THE BRAIN

Heavenly Father,

By the authority and power given to me by the holy name of our Lord Jesus Christ, I bind, break the soul-tie, break your power and cast out of me: the spirit of Post-Traumatic Stress Disorder, the strongmen of infirmity and death, destruction, and all other demonic spirits that are associated with this disorder. I demand that you leave me now as you have no legal right to stay. Go to the arid places and never return. Holy Spirit please fill every void place left by the departed spirits.

Lord, I ask you to destroy all the roots and seeds of this disorder. As you know, I have been severely traumatized. My brain and body are not working as they should. I pray for you to touch my brain and body, and restore the following to a normal condition:

I decree that my amygdala can learn to relax, and it will not be over stimulated.

I decree that my hippocampus can resume proper memory consolidation. It will return to normal size, and I will have growth of new neurons. It will not be under active.

I decree that my nervous system can recommence its easy flow between reactive and restorative modes.

I decree that my neurochemical systems including Cortisol and Norepinephrine will return to normal.

I decree that my body and brain will achieve a state of neutrality, and that you will reprogram my body and mind.

I decree that my family and friends will finally be at peace and have joy in their lives. Thank you, Lord. Amen.

PART IV

Spoken Word, Word Scriptures, Who You are In Christ, Spiritual Authority

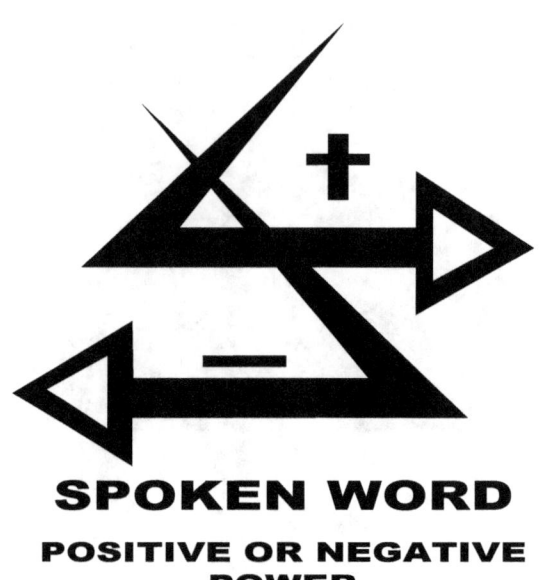

SPOKEN WORD
POSITIVE OR NEGATIVE POWER

Little Sparrow Ministries
©2001LittleSparrowMinistries

Words can bring either life (blessings) or death (curses). In Deuteronomy 11:26-29, the word of God states:

"...See, I am setting before you today a blessing and a curse – the blessing if you obey the commands of the Lord your God that I am giving you today; the curse if you disobey the commands of the Lord your God and turn from the way that I command you today...."

If we carefully scrutinize our vocabulary, we can determine where we are spiritually. Are we bringing God's truth into the world by speaking positively or are we bringing in the enemy's darkness by speaking negatively?

Our behavior or actions usually follow our spoken words, and our spoken words reveal the true condition of our hearts.

Matthew 12:34-37 *... for out of the overflow of the heart the mouth speaks. The good man brings good things out of the good stored up in him, and the evil man brings evil things out of the evil stored up in him. But I tell you that men will have to give account on the Day of Judgment for every careless word they have spoken. For by your words you will be acquitted, and by your words you will be condemned.*

We can determine if we are bearing good or bad fruit. Are the relationships with our family and friends healthy? Do we walk in peace and joy? But most of all is God's love the center of our lives? Does it flow from God through you to everyone around you?

Matthew 7:17-20 *Likewise every good tree bears good fruit, but a bad tree bears bad fruit. A good tree cannot bear bad fruit, and a bad tree cannot bear good fruit. Thus, by their fruit you will recognize them.*

As we speak positive and edifying words, we confirm the word of God in our lives and in others. By combining the words of God spoken from our mouths, with godly love and our faith, no weapon of the enemy will be able to stand against us. As a result, we will say to the mountains (circumstances in our lives) "MOVE." Then we will see the hand of God working – for nothing is impossible with our Lord. We should also keep our eyes fixed on our Lord at all times; we need to open our ears to hear God's truths.

Speak healing scriptures to those who are sick. By speaking financial scriptures to those who are in need of finances, they are encouraged; and their faith is renewed. To families that are torn apart from the actions of their own behaviors and the strategies of the enemy, speak of godly family relationships; and speak of scriptural forgiveness. Ask for God's intervention (his will) to be accomplished.

John 15:7-8 *If you remain in me and my words remain in you, ask whatever you wish, and it will be given you. This is to my Father's glory, that you bear much fruit, showing yourselves to be my disciples.*

Isaiah 55:11 ... *so is my word that goes out from my mouth. It will not return to me empty, but will accomplish what I desire and achieve the purpose for which I sent it.*

Negative words are harmful. How many times have we heard words from our parents, others, or yourself say:

"You will never amount to anything." "You will never be able to do this."

"You are stupid."

"Math is going to be as difficult for you as it was for me."

"You are not attractive or pretty." "No one will ever love you."

These negative and/or destructive remarks often become self-fulfilling prophecies.

The individual to whom the remarks were directed can internalize the destructive words. This internalization can govern their future behavior. As a result, Satan has gained a foothold in that person's life by establishing a seedbed of lies.

As soon as harmful remarks are spoken to me, I immediately rebuke them in the name of our Lord Jesus Christ. I DO NOT INTERNALIZE THEM. I recognize the source of these lies – Satan.

One example of this comes to my mind. My husband and I were at the doctor's office for a consultation.

My husband had some tests performed, and we were there for the results.

He had been diagnosed with cancer, and the doctor immediately gave us all the options available to us. Most were extremely negative and grim. However, my husband took my hand, and he said, "Honey, we have a greater Physician. I know there is a better way." When we left the doctor's office, we immediately came into a prayer of agreement; we rebuked all the negative words; we spoke positive words into the circumstances. God did heal my husband through an alternative medical procedure.

James 3:9-10 *With the tongue we praise our Lord and Father, and with it we curse men, who have been made in God's likeness. Out of the same mouth come praise and cursing. My brothers, this should not be.*

Wrongful prayers, gossip, and slander are examples of word curses. Prayers that try to control and manipulate someone according to another's fleshly desires are an abomination to God.

Psalm 52:2 *Your tongue plots destruction; it is like a sharpened razor, you who practice deceit. You love evil rather than good, falsehood rather than speaking the truth. You love every harmful word, O you deceitful tongue!*

The sin of murder is committed when one gossips or slanders another. They not only can kill a person's reputation, but they also can physically harm them. The following are several examples of how this sin, committed by others, can affect you.

One morning at home, I dropped something on the floor. As I picked it up, I felt the pain of a knife thrust into my back. The pain in the physical realm was overwhelming. I cried out, "God what is this?" He said, "gossip and slander." The Lord told me who spoke the curse. Immediately, I rebuked this pain and stated:

"By the authority and power given to me by the holy name of our Lord Jesus Christ, I demand this word curse, assignment, judgment, witchcraft, jealousy, envy, strife and every scheme and plan of the enemy to be broken and shattered. I demand that all strongmen and demonic spirits that were associated with these curses to leave me now and go to the arid places." I then asked the Lord to send blessings and conviction to the originator."

Within a few hours, most of the pain associated with that curse had disappeared.

Proverbs 12:18 *Reckless words pierce like a sword, but the tongue of the wise brings healing.*

For about two months, I had been sick. Several prescriptions of antibiotics had been prescribed for me, and it seemed that nothing was helping. In fact, I felt my life was being systematically taken from me.

I inquired of the Lord as to what was going on. The Holy Spirit revealed to me that it was a stronghold, and He specifically told me to call a certain intercessor. I immediately went to her office. As she prayed, the Lord revealed that a word curse had been spoken. We were both given revelation concerning the person who spoke the curse. After breaking the stronghold, I was 70% better within a few hours.

Proverbs 10:18-21 *He who conceals his hatred has lying lips, and whoever spreads slander is a fool. When words are many, sin is not absent, but he who holds his tongue is wise. The tongue of the righteous is choice silver, but the heart of the wicked is of little value. The lips of the righteous nourish many, but fools die for lack of judgment.*

When I pray for others, the Holy Spirit reveals curses that have been placed through revelation. As a result of these revelations, we come into a prayer of agreement; we break all the curses and/or strongholds.

1 Corinthians 4:12-13 *When we are cursed, we bless; when we are persecuted, we endure it; when we are slandered, we answer kindly.*

In order to see the hand of God work, we must forgive those who have harmed us. Do not let a root of bitterness develop.

Ephesians 4:31-32 *Get rid of all bitterness, rage and anger, brawling and slander, along with every form of malice. Be kind and compassionate to one another, forgiving each other, just as in Christ, God forgave you.*

If you need to forgive someone, please go to the Forgiveness Prayer on page 13.

We can so easily be caught up in the snare of Satan's web. For example, I was making an overnight road trip with another Christian. We began speaking about many things – casually and without much thought. All of a sudden I felt grief and sorrow. The Lord told me I had grieved the Holy Spirit with my gossiping. I immediately repented, and I asked for forgiveness. However, the grief continued in my spirit; it seemed forever.

In order to prevent future sin in my life and the grieving of the Holy Spirit, I lift to the Lord my conversations that concern others. I ask him to forgive me if I have committed a sin, knowingly or unknowingly.

There is a fine line I must walk between discernment in ministry and gossip. I have asked God for the gift of discernment and wisdom.

1 Peter 3:10 *For whoever would love life and see good days must keep his tongue from evil and his lips from deceitful speech.*

Remember that the battleground between light and darkness is in the mind. Often in the midst of the battle our minds may become confused. Confusion is not of God.

1 Corinthians 14:33 *For God is not a God of disorder but of peace.*

Confusion can be the result of a number of weapons used by the enemy. There are at least two strongmen that can bring confusion - lying spirits and fear. Also, word curses can bring confusion.

The strongman of lying spirits can bring confusion to your mind as a result of lies being stated around you, to you, and in the form of wrongful prayers and word curses. When the strongman of fear gains a foothold in your life, one of the side effects is confusion to the point of complete immobilization.

At one point in my life, after the death of my first husband, I became so fearful that only by the grace of God was I able to get out of bed. I could not take care of my son and myself. I couldn't even balance my checkbook. Confusion reigned in my life. If I had been spiritually mature during that time of my life, I would have known what to do. However, my blessed Savior took over my life; He kept my son and me from harm.

Should this happen to you, demand that the lying spirit, spirit of fear, and spirit of confusion to leave; send them to the arid places, and never return.

I now ask you through your spoken words to let the positive power of godly love flow through you.

"Lord, I ask that everyone who reads these words have ears to hear and eyes to see spiritual truths."

"Lord, I ask that your words penetrate your children's innermost being so that their words are always positive, and they speak your truths."

"Lord, I ask that you bring your children to a new level of spiritual maturity."

"Lord, I ask that your children always speak blessings over themselves and others, and that they will see with spiritual eyes your mighty hand working in their lives."

WORD SCRIPTURES

It was the speaking forth of his word that brought creation into being:

Gen. 1:11 ... *and God said let the land produce vegetation... And it was so.*

Gen 1:14 ...*and God said let there be light... And it was so.*

Gen. 1:20 ...*and God said, let the water teem with living creatures... So God created.*

Gen. 1:24 ... *and God said let the land produce living creatures... And it was so.*

Mark 11:23-24 *I tell you the truth, if anyone says to this mountain, 'Go throw yourself into the sea,' and does not doubt in his heart but believes that what he says will happen, it will be done for him. Therefore I tell you, whatever you ask for in prayer, believe that you have received it, and it will be yours.*

Ephesians 5:1 *Therefore, be imitators of God...*

WHO YOU ARE IN CHRIST

1 Peter 1:23 *I am God's child, born again of the incorruptible seed.*

Matthew 5:13 *I am the salt of the earth.*

John 8:31-33 *I am set free.*

John 17:11 *I am protected by the power of his name.*

John 17:15 *I am kept from the evil one.*

Romans 5:1 *I am at peace with God.*

Romans 6:11 *I am dead to sin and alive to God in Christ Jesus.*

Romans 6:14 *I am free from the power of sin.*

Romans 8:37 *I am more than a conqueror through Christ.*

2 Corinthians 12:9 *I am the strongest when I am weakest.*

Ephesians 1:4 *I am chosen by God to be holy and blameless.*

Ephesians 4:13 *I am becoming mature, the measure of the stature of the fullness of Christ.*

Colossians 1:29 *I am filled with God's power that works mightily in me.*

Revelation 21:7 *I am victorious.*

HALLELUJAH, HALLELUJAH, HALLELUJAH

SPIRITUAL AUTHORITY

Luke 9:1   *When Jesus had called the twelve together, he gave them power and authority to drive out all demons and to cure diseases, and he sent them out to preach the kingdom of God and to heal the sick.*

Luke: 10:19   *...I have given you authority to trample on snakes and scorpions (demons and evil spirits) and to overcome all the power of the enemy; nothing will harm you.*

Ephesians 6:14-28   *...In addition to all this, take up the shield of faith, with which you can extinguish all the flaming arrows of the evil one....*

Matthew 10:1   *He called his twelve disciples to him and gave them authority to drive out evil spirits and to heal every disease and sickness.*

Matthew 28:18   *All authority in heaven and earth has been given to me. God himself is the power behind our authority. (The devil and his forces are obliged to recognize our authority.)*

Acts 1:8 *But you will receive power when the Holy Spirit comes on you; and you will be my witnesses in Jerusalem, and in all Judea and Samaria, and to the ends of the earth.*

Proverbs 18:21 *The tongue has the power of life and death.*

God has given us the power and authority to drive out evil spirits and to heal every disease and sickness. The **tongue** is the weapon to be used to demonstrate this power and authority. The enemy cannot hear our thoughts. Praying a prayer in silence renders it ineffective. We must verbally address the enemy. The **prayer of agreement** is another weapon to be used with the **tongue**.

Know, without a doubt, that the Holy Spirit has come upon you, and has given you the power and authority to deal with the enemy. Stand firm and resist; he will flee.

Kenneth Hagin states in his book, ***The Believer's Authority***, "All the authority that can be exercised upon the earth has to be exercised through the Church, because Christ is not here in person – in his physical body. We are the Body of Christ. Even though we have prayed, 'Now Lord, you do this and that,' leaving everything up to him. He has conferred his authority on the earth to his Body, the

Church. Thus, many problems exist because we permit them to. We are not doing anything about them. We are the ones who are supposed to do something about them, but we are trying to get someone else, including God, to do something about them." Use your authority!

We must be specific in our prayers. The following is an example. This situation happened in the beginning of my ministry. Since then, I hope and pray that I have learned how to use God's weapons to protect myself. Thank God for his grace and mercy.

One evening the Lord told me to go to the church. Of course, I immediately left and walked up to the second floor of the building. A woman I had previously been counseling was walking towards me. She stated she had been praying that I would come. Her body was in the beginning stages of Multiple Sclerosis. She was having a difficult time walking. I began taking authority over the spirit of infirmity. I was on my knees praying over her legs, and a spirit jumped on me. I could not raise my right arm. I spoke to the spirit of infirmity and demanded it leave me. It would not leave. The lady left walking straighter; however, I was in terrible shape.

When I got home, I asked God why I couldn't get rid of this spirit. He said, "You did not speak to the spirit of Multiple Sclerosis." I immediately cast off that spirit. The spirit of infirmity is a strongman. I addressed the strongman and the individual spirit of Multiple Sclerosis. I was specific, and it had to leave. It did.

Another example: Let us take "anger." Anger is a spirit under the strongman of jealousy. Address the strongman of jealousy and spirit of anger. Cast it out.

You can cast it out of yourself but cannot cast it out of another person unless they are a willing participant. They must verbally tell it to flee. If that individual is not willing to participate, the only thing you can do is bind that spirit; and you can loosen the Holy Spirit to bring him truth and knowledge so that he may be set free.

PART V

Prayers: Discouragement, Fear/Anxiety/Worry, Grief, Guilt/Shame, Harassing and Tormenting Spirits, Heaviness/Depression/Suicidal Thoughts, Horrifying Thoughts and Dreams, Mental Strongholds, Oppression, Peace, Protection, Trust

DISCOURAGEMENT

Joshua 1:9   *Have I not commanded you? Be strong and courageous. Do not be terrified; do not be discouraged, for the Lord your God will be with you wherever you go.*

1 Peter 5:7   *Cast all your anxiety on him because he cares for you.*

Psalms 55:22   *Cast your cares on the Lord and he will sustain you; he will never let the righteous fall.*

Nahum 1:7   *The Lord is good, a refuge in times of trouble. He cares for those who trust in him.*

Psalms 97:12   *Rejoice in the Lord, you who are righteous, and praise his holy name.*

Psalms 104:31   *May the glory of the Lord endure forever; may the Lord rejoice in his works…*

Psalms 104:34   *May my meditation be pleasing to him, as I rejoice in the Lord.*

PLEASE PRAY OUT LOUD.

Heavenly Father,

I am discouraged because I do not see circumstances changing. I know faith is believing in things that are unseen. Please, Lord, increase my faith.

In the name of Jesus, I bind, break the soul-tie, break your power, and cast out of me: the strongmen of heaviness, fear and lying spirits, as well as the spirit of discouragement, dormant spirits, familiar spirits, and familial spirits. I demand that you separate from me now. Holy Spirit please fill all the void places left by the departing spirits. I loosen right thinking and joy in my life.

I know that you are in control of my life, and the Holy Spirit will guide and direct me. I will put on the garment of praise for the spirit of heaviness. I will rejoice in the Lord, and praise his holy name. Amen

FEAR /ANXIETY/WORRY

Romans 8:15 *For you did not receive a spirit of slavery to fall back into fear, but you received the Spirit of adoption, by whom we cry out, "Abba, Father!"*

Hebrews 13:6 *So we say with confidence, the Lord is my helper, and I will not be afraid. What can man do to me?*

1 John 4:18 *There is no fear in love. But perfect love drives out fear, because fear has to do with punishment. The one who fears is not made perfect in love.*

Proverbs 3:25-26 *Have no fear of sudden disaster or of the ruin that overtakes the wicked, for the Lord will be your confidence and will keep your foot from being snared.*

Psalms 23:4 *Even though I walk through the valley of the shadow of death, I will fear no evil, for you are with me; your rod and your staff they comfort me.*

Psalms 27:1-3 *The Lord is my light and my salvation - whom shall I fear? The Lord is the stronghold of my life - of whom shall I be afraid? When evil men advance against me to devour my flesh, when my enemies and my foes attack me, they will stumble and fall.*

Psalms 56:11   *In God I trust; I will not be afraid. What can man do to me?*

Isaiah 41:13   *For I am the Lord, your God, who takes hold of your right hand and says to you, "Do not fear; I will help you."*

John 14:*27*   *Peace I leave with you, my peace I give you; I do not give to you as the world gives. Do not let your hearts be troubled and do not be afraid.*

God's love will remove all fear. However, we must make a decision not to entertain fearful thoughts. We must **TRUST** God in all things.

PLEASE PRAY OUT LOUD.

Heavenly Father,

In the name of Jesus, I bind, break the soul-ties, break your power, and cast out of me: the strongmen of fear and lying spirits, as well as the spirits of anxiety, confusion, dormant spirits, familiar spirits, and familial spirits. I demand you to separate from me now. You have no legal right to stay. Go to the arid places, and never return. Do not attach yourself to anyone or anything.

Holy Spirit, I ask that you fill every void place left by the departing spirits. Fill me with your peace. Please take my mind captive so that it is filled with trust, faith, and belief.

I surrender the situation of _____ to you. I no longer will carry this burden because it is now on your shoulders. Amen.

GRIEF

Psalms 34:18   *The Lord is close to the brokenhearted; he rescues those who are crushed in spirit.*

Matthew 5:4   *Blessed are they that mourn for they shall be comforted.*

Luke 6:21   *...Blessed are you that weep now for you will laugh.*

Psalms 147:3   *He heals the brokenhearted and binds up their wounds.*

Proverbs 15:13   *A happy heart makes the face cheerful, but heartache crushes the spirit.*

Revelation 21:4   *He will wipe every tear from their eyes. There will be no more death or mourning or crying or pain, for the old order of things has passed away.*

PLEASE PRAY OUT LOUD.

Heavenly Father,

In the name of Jesus, I bind, break the soul-ties, break your powers, and cast out of me the strongman of heaviness and the spirits of grief and sorrow. I demand you to separate from me now. Go to the arid places, and never return. Do not attach yourselves to anyone or anything. Holy Spirit fill every void place left by the departing spirits.

In the name of Jesus, I ask you to sever the soul-tie with _____ (person). I ask that you heal and restore all the fragmented pieces of my soul. I also ask you to heal my body and spirit.

Take my mind and emotions captive. I decree that you are healing my broken heart and my emotional wounds. I decree the Lord is restoring my joy.

Psalms 30:11 *You turned my wailing into dancing. You removed my sackcloth and clothed me with joy.* Amen.

GUILT/SHAME

Psalms 32:1 *Blessed is he whose transgressions are forgiven, whose sins are covered.*

Psalms 32:5 *Then I acknowledged my sin to you and did not cover up my iniquity. I said, "I will confess my transgressions to the Lord" – and you forgave the guilt of my sin. "Selah."*

Psalms 39:8 *Save me from all my transgressions; do not make me the scorn of fools.*

Psalms 103:12 *As far as the east is from the west, so far has he removed our transgressions from us.*

Isaiah 43:25 *I, even I, am he who blots out your transgressions, for my own sake, and remembers your sins no more.*

John 1:9 *If we confess our sins, he is faithful and just and will forgive us our sins and purify us from all unrighteousness.*

PLEASE PRAY OUT LOUD.

Heavenly Father,

In the name of Jesus, I bind, break the soul-ties, break your power, and cast out of me the strongmen of lying spirits and the spirit of bondage as well as the familiar spirits, familial spirits, and dormant spirits. I demand you to separate from me now. Go to the arid places, and never return. Do not attach yourselves to anyone or anything. Holy Spirit fill every void place left by the departing spirits.

Through the grace and mercy of Jesus Christ, I am saved, and my sins are not remembered. He has blotted out my transgression, and I am forgiven. If Jesus can forgive me, then I must forgive myself. I will no longer listen to the lies of the enemy. I have been purified from all unrighteousness; I trust in him and will never be put to shame. I am a child of the Most High. Thank you, Lord. Amen.

HARRASSING AND TORMENTING SPIRITS

2 Corinthians 12:7 ...*there was given me a thorn in my flesh, a messenger of Satan, to torment me....*

1 Samuel 16:15 *Saul's attendants said to him, "See an evil spirit from God is tormenting you."*

1 Samuel 16:14 *Now the Spirit of the Lord had departed from Saul, and an evil spirit from the Lord tormented him.*

Matthew 15:22 *A Canaanite woman from that vicinity came to him, crying out, "Lord, Son of David, have mercy on me! My daughter is suffering terribly from demon-possession."*

Several of the above scriptures state that the Lord sent a tormenting spirit. These statements and similar ones in scripture indicate that evil spirits are subject to God's control. Therefore, we must at all times be obedient to God's word and be in right standing with him.

If we have surrendered our lives to him, the Lord will use us to advance his kingdom. Therefore, we are a threat to Satan. The enemy will use every weapon at its disposal. The harassing and tormenting spirits are included in its arsenal of weapons. These spirits can manifest in a number of ways. Some of the manifestations include sharp pains in the body, headaches, and oppression. They usually are stubborn spirits; use your authority. Whatever weapon the enemy is using such as the strongmen of heaviness, fear, or lying spirits, use your authority; get rid of them.

PLEASE PRAY OUT LOUD.

Heavenly Father,

In the name of Jesus, I bind, break the soul-ties, break your power, and cast out of me the harassing and tormenting spirits. I demand you to separate from me now. Go to the arid places, and never return. Get out of my home and property. Do not attach yourselves to anyone or anything. Holy Spirit fill every void place left by the departing spirits.

I declare and decree that my mind and body are free from harassing and tormenting spirits. I declare and decree that my joy has returned. Amen.

HEAVINESS/DEPRESSION/ SUICIDAL THOUGHTS

Isaiah 53:4   *Surely he took up our infirmities and carried our sorrows.*

Nehemiah 8:10   *Do not grieve, for the joy of the Lord is your strength.*

Psalms 34:7   *The angel of the Lord encamps around those that fear him, and he delivers them.*

Isaiah 61:3   *...and provide for those who grieve in Zion – to bestow on them a crown of beauty instead of ashes, the oil of gladness instead of mourning, and a garment of praise instead of a spirit of despair.*

Romans: 12:21   *Do not be overcome by evil, but overcome evil with good.*

PLEASE PRAY OUT LOUD.

Heavenly Father,

I have allowed the strongman of heaviness to rob me of the good things you have for me. I promise to reject those negative thoughts and to make praise to you a way of life from this time forth.

In the name of Jesus, I bind, break the soul-ties, break your power, and cast out of me: the strongmen of heaviness and familiar spirits, spirits of depression, excessive mourning, sorrow, grief, broken heart, despair, dejection, self-pity, insomnia, rejection, hopelessness, suicidal thoughts, inner hurts, torn spirit, familial spirits, and dormant spirits. I demand you to separate from me now. Go to the arid places, and never return. Holy Spirit please come and fill every void place left by the departing spirits.

I loosen right thinking and truth. I loosen the Comforter, which is the Holy Spirit, the garment of praise, and the oil of joy.

Lord, I declare and decree that I am healed and you have restored all the fragmented pieces of my soul. Amen.

HORRIFYING THOUGHTS AND DREAMS

Palms 139:23 *Search me, O God, and know my heart; test me and know my anxious thoughts.*

Proverbs 15:26 *The Lord detests the thoughts of the wicked, but those of the pure are pleasing to him.*

Isaiah 26:3 *You will keep in perfect peace him whose mind is steadfast because he trusts in you.*

A tactic of the enemy is to bombard us with horrifying thoughts and dreams. Dreams from the enemy are most often in black and white; they usually are horrifying in nature. God does not give us horrifying dreams. Discern that they are from the enemy; deal with the situation immediately! Do not let evil thoughts get a stronghold in your mind. Rebuke the thoughts, and ask God to take your mind captive. Do not condemn yourself.

PLEASE PRAY OUT LOUD.

Heavenly Father,

In the name of Jesus, I bind, break the soul-ties, break your power, and cast out of me the strongman of lying spirits and harassing and tormenting spirits. I demand you to separate from me now. Go to the arid places, and never return. You cannot attach yourself to anyone or anything.

Your tentacles that have been placed around my mind are severed by the Sword of the Spirit. No weapon will be able to form against me. I decree that my thoughts are pure and holy. Lord, I ask that you take my mind captive. I plead the blood over myself, and I ask you to place a hedge of fire around my mind and release peace and joy.

I prophetically decree that when the enemy tries to gain access to my mind, I will immediately rebuke those impure or horrifying thoughts. Amen.

MENTAL STRONGHOLDS

Romans 12:2 *Do not conform any longer to the pattern of this world, but be transformed by the renewing of your mind. Then you will be able to test and approve what God's will is - his good, pleasing, and perfect will.*

2 Corinthians 10:4-5 *The weapons we fight with are not the weapons of the world. On the contrary, they have divine power to demolish strongholds. We demolish arguments and every pretension that sets itself up against the knowledge of God, and we take captive every thought to make it obedient to Christ.*

Romans 8:6 *The mind of the sinful man is death, but the mind controlled by the Spirit is life and peace.*

Isaiah 26:3 *You will keep in perfect peace him whose mind is steadfast, because he trusts in you.*

2 Timothy 1:7 *For God did not give us a spirit of timidity, but a spirit of power, of love and self-discipline.*

PLEASE PRAY OUT LOUD.

Heavenly Father,

I am having trouble keeping my mind in perfect peace. The enemy is creating mine fields in my mind, and as a result confusion reigns. If there are strongholds in my life that need to be destroyed, guide and direct me so that I can shut these open doors. If there is a forgiveness problem, convict me.

In the name of Jesus, I bind, break the soul-ties, break your power, and cast out of me: the strongmen of dumb and deaf spirits, lying spirits, familiar spirits, fear, and heaviness, the spirits of mental illness, insanity, suicide, crying, familial spirits, dormant spirits, and confusion. I demand that you separate from me now. Go to the arid places, and never return. Holy Spirit please fill all void places left by the departing spirits. I loosen right thinking and perfect peace.

I ask for a hedge of fire around my mind and emotions. I will walk in perfect peace knowing that the Holy Spirit is in complete control of my mind. I prophetically decree that I have a spirit of power, of love, and a sound mind. Amen.

OPPRESSION

Psalms 34:17   *The righteous cry out, and the Lord hears them; he delivers them from all their troubles.*

Psalms 9:9   *The Lord also is a refuge for the oppressed, a stronghold in times of trouble.*

Psalms 18:17   *He rescued me from my powerful enemy, from my foes, who were too strong for me.*

Acts 10:38   *How God anointed Jesus of Nazareth with the Holy Ghost and power; and how he went about doing good and healing all that were under the power of the devil, because God was with him.*

Psalms 12:5   *Because of the oppression of the weak and the groaning of the needy, I will now arise, says the Lord. "I will protect them from those who malign them."*

Isaiah 43:2   *When you pass through waters, I will be with you. And when you pass through the rivers, they will not sweep over you. When you walk through the fire, you will not be burned; the flames will not set you a blaze.*

PLEASE PRAY OUTLOUD.

Heavenly Father,

By the power and authority that my Lord Jesus Christ has given me, I bind, break the soul-ties, break your power, and cast out of me: the spirits of oppression, depression, heaviness, familiar spirits, familial spirits, harassing spirits, and tormenting spirits. I demand you to separate from me now. Go to the arid places, and never return. You cannot attach yourself to anyone or anything. Holy Spirit please fill all the void places left by the departing spirits.

Your evil tentacles that invaded my mind are severed by the Sword of the Spirit. *"I will lie down in peace and sleep, for you alone, O Lord, will keep me safe."* (Psalms 4:8)

Holy Spirit, please fill me from the top of my head to the souls of my feet with peace and joy. Lord, release your ministering angels to encamp around me. Surround me with a hedge of fire so that the lies and darts of the enemy cannot harass and torment my body, soul, and spirit. Amen.

PEACE

John 16:33 *I have told you these things, so that in me you may have peace. In this world, you will have trouble. But take heart! I have overcome the world.*

Luke 2:14 *Glory to God in the highest, and on earth peace to men on whom his favor rests.*

Luke 1:79 *...to shine on those living in darkness and in the shadow of death, to guide our feet into the path of peace.*

Galatians 5:22 *But the fruit of the Spirit is: love, joy, peace, patience, kindness, goodness, faithfulness, gentleness, and self-control.*

2 Corinthians 13:11 *Finally, brothers and sisters, good-by. Aim for perfection, listen to my appeal, be of one mind, live in peace. And the God of love and peace will be with you.*

Romans 8:6 *The mind of sinful man is death, but the mind controlled by the Spirit is life and peace.*

PLEASE PRAY OUT LOUD.

Heavenly Father,

In the name of Jesus, I bind, break the soul-ties, break your power, and cast out of me the strongmen of lying spirits and fear as well as tormenting and harassing spirits. I demand you to separate from me now. Go to the arid places never to return. You cannot attach yourself to anyone or anything.

Holy Spirit cover me with your peace as the enemy has overwhelmed me with fear, doubt, and unbelief. I prophetically decree that *the God of peace will soon crush Satan under my feet, and that the grace of our Lord Jesus Christ is with me.* (Romans 16:20) I also decree *that the Holy Spirit controls my mind where there is life and peace.* (Romans 8:6) And *the peace you give isn't like the peace the world gives. I will not be troubled or afraid.* (John 14:27) Amen.

PROTECTION

2 Thessalonians 3:3 *But the Lord is faithful, and he will strengthen and protect you from the evil one.*

1 Peter 5:7 *Cast all your anxiety on him because he cares for you.*

Luke 10:19 *And I have given you authority to trample on snakes and scorpions and to overcome all the power of the enemy; nothing will harm you.*

Proverbs 1:33 *... but whoever listens to me will live in safety and be at ease, without fear of harm.*

Psalms 7:10 *My shield is God Most High, who saves the upright in heart.*

Psalms 5:12 *For surely, O Lord, you bless the righteous; you surround them with your favor as with a shield.*

Psalms 57:2-3 *I cry out to God Most High, to God, who fulfills his purpose for me. He sends from heaven and saves me, rebuking those who hotly pursue me; God sends his love and his faithfulness.*

Psalms 34:7 *For the angel of the Lord encamps around those who fear him, and he delivers them.*

Psalms 145:20 *The Lord watches over all who love him, but all the wicked he will destroy.*

Psalms 121:7-8 *The Lord keeps you from all harm – he will watch over your life; the Lord will watch over your coming and going both now and forevermore.*

Psalms 138:7 *Though I walk in the midst of trouble, you preserve my life; you stretch out your hand against the anger of my foes, with your right hand you save me.*

PLEASE PRAY OUT LOUD.

Heavenly Father,

In the name of Jesus, I pray that you would protect me from bacterial or viral infections, diseases, or other infirmities that would try to kill, steal, or destroy my body. I ask for your right hand to save me from accidents, dangers, plans, and schemes of the enemy.

Be my fortress, strength, shield, and stronghold. Make me to dwell and if necessary hide in the shadow of your wings. Be my rock, salvation, and defense so that I will not be moved or shaken.

Lord, I am asking for the gift of discernment, and wisdom that will preserve me from all evil.

I demand that all forms of evil communication are severed, and the demonic spirits are rendered deaf and dumb.

I will use mightily all the heavenly power and authority available to me to tread on serpents and scorpions and over all the power of the enemy.

I will stand firm and resist the devil. The enemy will flee at the sound of the Sword of the Spirit as it springs forth from my mouth. It will be as rushing waters filled with life and truth. There is no weapon formed against me that will succeed. Amen.

TRUST

1 John 4:16　*And so we know and rely on the love God has for us. God is love. Whoever lives in love lives in God, and God in him.*

1 Peter 1:8　*Though you have not seen him, you love him; and even though you do not see him now, you believe in him and are filled with an inexpressible and glorious joy,*

Psalm 9:10　*Those who know your name trust in you; for you, Lord, have never forsaken those who seek you.*

Psalm 13:5　*But I trust in your unfailing love; my heart rejoices in your salvation.*

Psalm 20:7　*Some trust in chariots and some in horses, but we trust in the name of the Lord our God.*

Psalm 22:4　*In you, our ancestors put their trust; they trusted and you delivered them.*

Proverbs 3:5　*Trust in the Lord with all your heart and lean not on your own understanding; in all your ways acknowledge him, and he will make your paths straight.*

PLEASE PRAY OUT LOUD.

Heavenly Father,

In the name of Jesus, I bind, break the soul-ties, break your power, and cast out of me the strongmen of fear and lying spirits. I demand you to separate from me now. Go to the arid places, and never return. You cannot attach yourself to anyone or anything.

Lord, I ask you to increase my trust in you. May my roots go down deep into the rich soil of your marvelous love. I ask for a hedge of protection around my mind and thoughts.

I will no longer listen to the lying spirits. As the lies enter my thoughts, I will rebuke them immediately. There will only be positive words that flow from my mouth because *"...for out of the overflow of the heart the mouth speaks."* (Luke 6:45) My faith and hope are now placed confidently in you. Amen.

BOOKS AND REFERENCES STUDIED

Generational Bondages/Curses

1. *Merriam-Webster's Collegiate Dictionary* 1994, 1995

2. Rebecca Brown, M.D., *Unbroken Curses*, (New Kensington, PA: Whitaker House, 1995)

Bitterness

1. *Merriam-Webster's Online Dictionary* Copyright © 2005 by Merriam-Webster, Incorporated

2. Pastor Jess Little, *Removing the Root of Bitterness,* Trinity Baptist Church, Moscow, ID

Cover painting by Judith H. Farris-Smith

Forgiveness

1. Dr. Charles Stanley, **The Gift of Forgiveness** (Nashville, TN: Thomas Nelson Publishing)

2. John Bevere, **The Bait of Satan** (Lake Mary, FL: Creation House, 1994)

Occult

1. David Benoit, *Who's Watching the Playpen?* (Oklahoma City, OK: Hearthstone Publishing LTD, 1995) Used by permission.

4. Josh McDowell and Don Stewart, *Handbook of Today's Religions,* (Nashville, TN: Thomas Nelson Publishers 1993)

5. Selwyn Stevens, *The New Age, The Old Lie in a New Package* (Wellington, New Zealand: Jubilee Publishers, 1992, 1993, 1994, 1996, 1997)

6. Selwyn Stevens and Dr. Badu Bediako, *Treated or Tricked, Alternative Health Therapies Diagnosed* (Wellington, New Zealand: Jubilee Publishers, 1996, 1997, 2000)

7. *Webster's II New College Dictionary,* (Boston, MA: Houghton Mifflin Company, 1999, 1995) (Some definitions in Glossary are based on material from this dictionary.)

Offense

1. John Bevere, **The Bait of Satan** (Lake Mary, FL: Creation House, 1994)

PTSD

1. Viatcheslav Wlassoff, PhD, *How Does Post-Traumatic Stress Disorder Change The Brain?* 1-24-2015

2. J. Douglas Bremner, MD, *Traumatic Stress: Effects on the Brain.*

3. Psychcentral.com

4. National Center for Post-Traumatic Stress Disorder (2009), *What is PTSD?*

5. American Psychological Association (2000)

6. J. Briere (2009) *The Brain, Brain Chemistry, and PTS*. National Child Traumatic Stress Network, SAMHSA. University of Southern California

7. National Institute of Mental Health

8. Guidelines for Differential Diagnose in a Population with Post-Traumatic Stress Disorder

9. Journal of Professional Psychology Research and Practice

Salvation

1. Library of Ralph Wilkerson, *Kathryn Kuhlman's Healing Words*, (Orlando, FL: Creation House, 1997) Page 4

Soul-Ties

1. Bill and Sue Banks, *Breaking Unhealthy Soul-Ties*, (Kirkwood, MO: Impact Christian Books, Inc. 1999, 2001)

Spoken Word

1. Charles Capps, *The Tongue – A Creative Force*, (Tulsa, OK: Harrison House, Inc., 1995, 1976)

2. Francis Frangipane, *Three Battlegrounds* (Cedar Rapids, IA: Advancing Church Publications, 1989)

Strongmen

1. Dr. Carol Robeson, *Strongman's Name...What's His Game?* (Keizer, OR: Shiloh Publishing House, 1983, 1996)

Veterans

1. demonbusters.com/war
2. AllaboutGod.net
3. thelordmybanner.com/PTSD

OTHER BOOKS BY LITTLE SPARROW MINISTRIES

Setting Yourself Free, Deliverance from Darkness (Little Sparrow Ministries, Copyright © 2001, 2003, 2008, 2011, 2013, 2017 Lindale, Texas 75771)

Targeted Prayers (Little Sparrow Ministries, Copyright © 2005, 2008, 2011, 2012, 2017 Lindale, Texas 75771)

Set Yourself Free Little Children and Come to Me (Little Sparrow Ministries, Copyright © 2001, 2003, 2009, 2017 Lindale, Texas 75771)

Truth vs. Lies, Information for Teenagers (Little Sparrow Ministries, Copyright © 2007, 2008, 2014, 2017 Lindale, Texas 75771)

Little Bit, the Miracle Kid (Little Sparrow Ministries, Copyright © 2009 Lindale, Texas 75771)

Have Faith, Inspirational Testimonies (Little Sparrow Ministries, Copyright © 2011 Lindale, Texas 75771)

I Am Abused (Little Sparrow Ministries, Copyright © 2017 Lindale, Texas 75771)

Collection of Letters from the Father's Heart (Little Sparrow Ministries, Copyright © 2017 Lindale, Texas 75771)

Freedom (Little Sparrow Ministries, Copyright © 2017 Lindale, Texas 75771)

www.ingramcontent.com/pod-product-compliance
Lightning Source LLC
LaVergne TN
LVHW011720060526
838200LV00051B/2976